FOREWORD

Called 'the language of heaven', Welsh is beautiful to speak, fascinating to learn and enchanting to hear. It's a musical language, liltingly poetic, and has long been the language of the hearth. But it is also the language of school, office and government, and is equally at home in TV, film and pop culture.

The fact that it has changed so little over the last thousand years is living proof that it was near perfect in the first place! And living it is. Its resurgence and growing popularity over the last half a century are testament to the beauty of its sounds and the wealth of expression the language offers its speakers, native and learner alike. Welsh is strong enough to have adapted over time, borrowing from other societies as it went, but locked in its vocabulary and grammar are also centuries of our heritage, culture and unity. The language of Wales is the kernel of her identity, and every Welsh speaker is a proud Welsh speaker.

'O bydded i'r hen iaith barhau.'

Elin Manahan Thomas

First Impressions

Should you be making a speedy entrance, you'll need to know that the Welsh for Police is HEDDLU – literally, the peace-force.

Driving into Wales, from east to west along the A55, the A5 or the M4, the traveller cannot fail to notice the place-names which proclaim loudly and clearly that this is a different country. Along the A55 there will be signs to Yr Wyddgrug / Mold or merely Rhyl, while the motorway journey in the south takes one past Cas-gwent / Chepstow or simply Cwmbrân. These Welsh place-names fascinate newcomers to Wales. 'What do they mean?' is the predictable, often-asked question. But interpreting and translating the meanings of place-names is a notoriously tricky task. The passage of time, their oral transmission, changes in the conventions of spelling and a desire to make the unintelligible, intelligible have all conspired to transform many of the old original names.

The great Welsh scholar Professor Melville Richards spent a lifetime unravelling the mysteries of Welsh place-names. When fire broke out in his home in Llangrannog, his daughter recalls how he mustered an army of neighbours to carry his research papers to safety. After his untimely death in 1973 it transpired that he had, in those pre-computer days, amassed 330,000 slips of paper in 159 boxes, which filled an entire wall in his office as Professor of Welsh at Bangor University. Others have laboured diligently since then to complete his *magnum opus* and now there is an on-line data base and several volumes on Welsh place-names and their meanings.

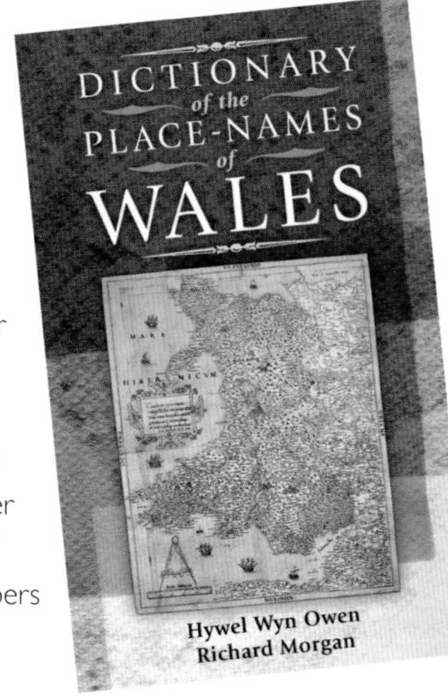

Place-names can offer the newcomer an introductory insight to the Welsh language. So many begin similarly – there are over 600 place-names beginning with *LLAN* (meaning church or enclosure); over 160 starting with *PEN* (head) and *TRE* (town, village or hamlet) and there are 90 *ABER*-s (estuary) listed in the gazetteer of Welsh place-names.

On a more intimate level Welsh house-names can also evoke historical meanings. *HENDRE* (winter dwelling) and *HAFOD* (summer dwelling) remind us of the medieval custom of transhumance, moving animals from summer to winter pastures. On farms, fields have their own names which have been passed down from generation to generation. A survey of field-names in Ardudwy, Merionethshire, recorded 1,000 farms with over 14,000 different field names, such as *Cae'r Odyn* (field of the kiln), *Dolafon* (river meadow) and *Parc Gwartheg* (cattle field).

The place-names of towns, villages, homes, farms, fields and also mountains and rivers are an essential element of the rich linguistic heritage of Wales. They should be protected and preserved.

Homes in Wales, even houseboats, will often have bilingual or Welsh names

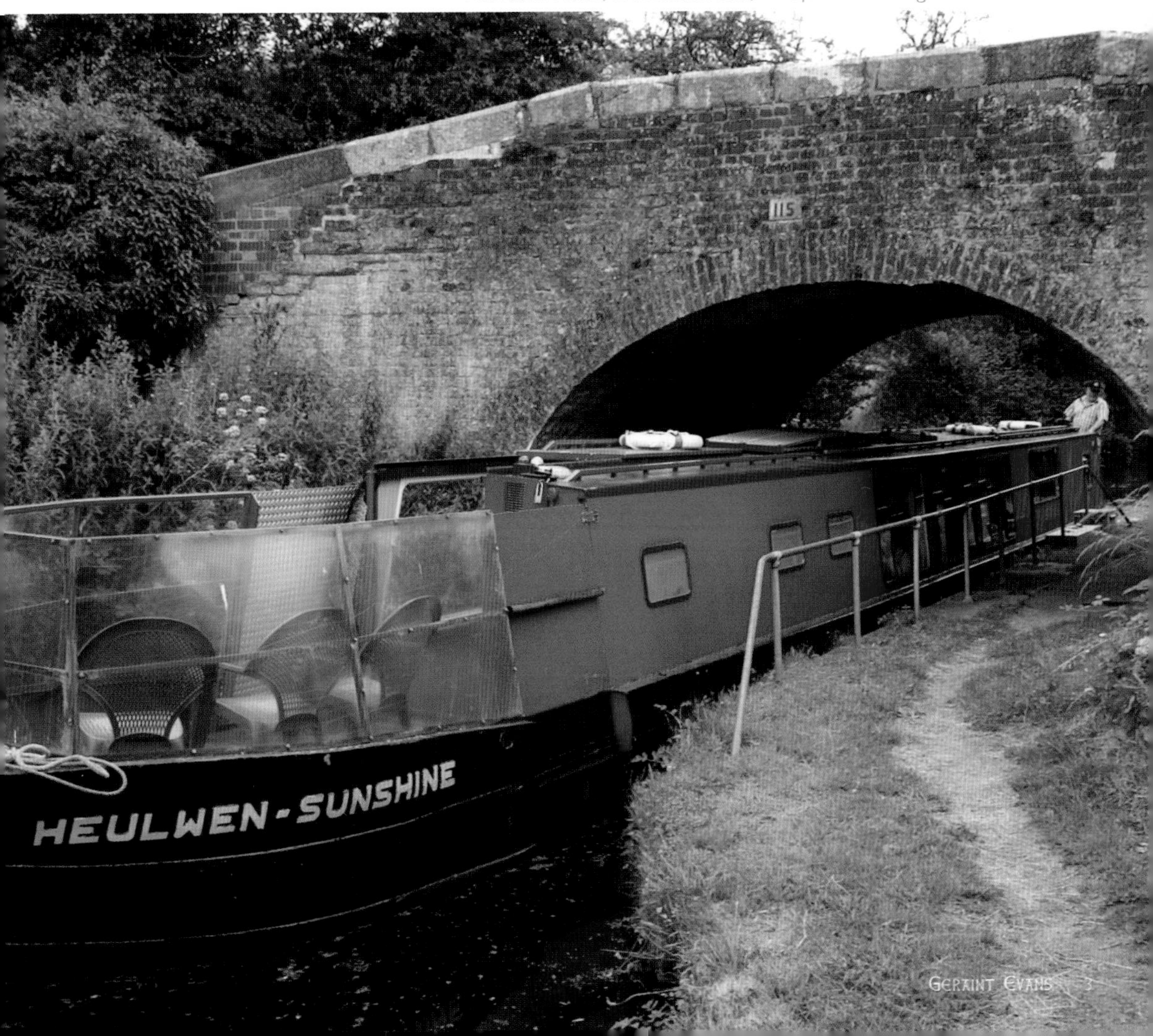

GERAINT EVANS

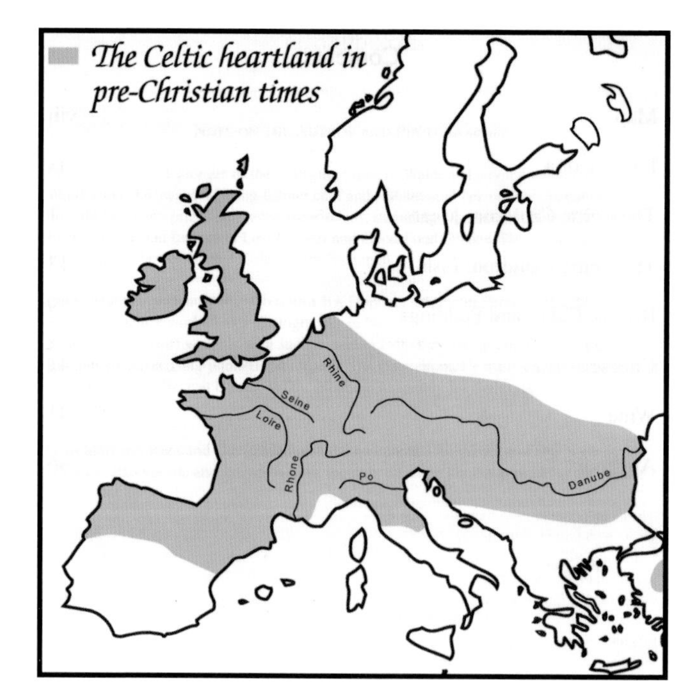

Where and when did it all begin?

The Welsh language is a member of the Celtic family of languages and today it is the most vibrant and frequently used member of this family. Although there is considerable controversy about the notion of a homogeneous Celtic people living in central and western Europe in pre-Roman times, there can be little doubt that these various 'Celtic' peoples spoke a common pan-Celtic tongue. The names of the rivers Rhone, Rhine and Danube are, for instance, Celtic in origin. The Gaulish Celts are recalled in Galipolli (city of the Gauls) in Turkey and in Galicia in the north of Spain today. This common Celtic tongue was itself derived from the ancient Indo-European family of languages.

From around 1000-600 BC the Celtic peoples began to arrive in Britain from the continent, bringing with them their distinctive art, religion and superb iron-making skills. It is probable that a form of Celtic was spoken over the whole of Britain at this time. Then, in the first century AD, the Romans arrived and for 400 years Britain was subjugated into the Roman Empire and its classical culture. Even then, Ireland, northern Scotland and parts of Wales were not fully integrated into the Empire and it is likely that forms of Celtic persisted in these areas. Gradually the mother tongue disintegrated into two main new families of languages: the Goedelic from which Irish, Gaelic and Manx evolved and in which the Indo-European sound 'kw' became 'q' and later 'c'; and the Brittonic where the 'kw' became 'p' and which formed the basis of the Welsh, Cornish, Cumbric and Breton languages. Thus, in some instances, the relationship between the Celtic tongues is obvious, in others the use of 'q' / 'p' emphasises the split from the mother Celtic.

With the Romans came the Latin tongue and it, in turn, contributed to the development of the Celtic/Britonnic language of Wales after the conquest and even for centuries afterwards, as it was the language of learning and of the early Christian church after the fall of the Roman empire. On the whole, the Britons borrowed Latin words for things which were unfamiliar to them and for words associated with the Christian faith, which was new to them. Thus *pont* (bridge) from the Latin pons; *lleng* (legion) from legio; *eglwys* (church) from ecclesia; *llyfr* (book) from libra; and *cannwyll* (candle) from candela are derived from the Latin and still in common usage today.

Relationships between Celtic Words:

Welsh	Breton	Irish	Gaelic	English
tŷ	ti	teach	tigh	house
ci	ki	cu	cu	dog
du	du	dubh	dubh	black
mab / ap		mac / mc		son

TWO GREAT SCHOLARS

Sir William 'Oriental' Jones (1746-94)

A mathematician, judge and polymath who studied the classics, many European languages and also Hebrew, Arabic and Persian and who served the British empire in Bengal, India for many years. In 1786 he famously declared that the languages of India and Europe were derived from the same source – now called Indo-European. This discovery has formed the basis of modern linguistic studies. Ironically, William Jones, although his family came from Anglesey, could not speak his mother tongue, Welsh, and it seems that he was introduced to the King of France as 'a man who speaks every language except his own'.

Edward Lhuyd (1660-1709)

A botanist and naturalist, and curator of the Ashmolean Museum in Oxford. As a result of his meticulous field studies into the antiquities, natural history and culture of Wales and his subsequent travels to research in other Celtic countries, he discovered for the first time the links between the different branches of the 'Celtic' family of languages. This pioneering study earned him the title of 'the father of comparative linguistics'.

Sculpture at the University of Wales Centre for Advanced Welsh and Celtic Studies, Aberystwyth

EARLY WELSH

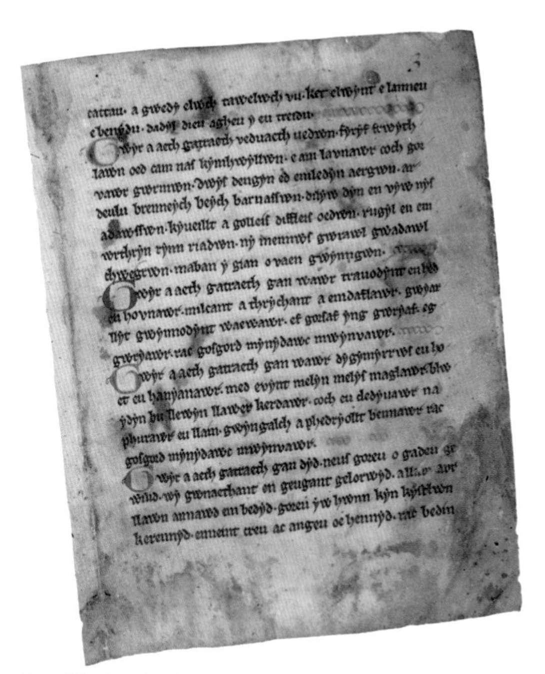

From The Book of Aneirin

With the retreat of the Roman army, c. 400 AD onwards, Britain entered a period of great upheaval and change. The frontiers were open to barbaric advances: the Angles and Saxons from the east and Irish marauders from the west. At this time the Brittonic tongue (the forerunner of Welsh) was spoken over most of southern Britain and in the northern kingdoms of *Ystrad Clud* (Strathclyde), *Rheged* (around modern Carlisle) and *Manaw Gododdin* (Edinburgh today). Gradually it evolved into separate tongues. The final syllables of Britonnic words were lost: bardos became *bardd* (bard); mapos – *mab* (son) and personal names such as Cunobelinos became Cynfelyn.

Meanwhile the new Welsh language which emerged was influenced by Irish too. Traces of this can be found in place-names such as Llŷn and Dinllaen in Gwynedd and in ordinary names such as *cerbyd* (vehicle) and *talcen* (forehead).

As the Anglo Saxons penetrated west, submerging the native Brittonic speakers in what is now England, Wales became defined as the land we know today. The Anglo Saxons called their neighbours 'Wealas' – 'Welsh' meaning foreigners or Romanised people; while the Welsh called themselves *Cymry*, from the Brittonic *combroges* – fellow countrymen, and their language *Cymraeg*. This new language can be said to have come into existence by c. 550 AD.

The evidence for early Welsh is scant and often difficult to interpret. It survives in inscriptions on memorials and in marginal notes in early documents. One of the most important early inscriptions is that carved on a memorial stone in Tywyn, Merionethshire – CINGEN CELEN TRIGET NITANAM which reads 'the body of Cingen dwells beneath' and was probably erected in c. 810 AD.

OLD WELSH

This is considered to be the second phase in the development of the Welsh language. The few sources which have survived are difficult to interpret. The *Surexit* fragment, for example, is the earliest known example of written syntactical Welsh. It records an ancient land dispute and has survived in the St Chad gospel book. The earliest surviving literary text is that of three '*englynion*' (short poems) found in the *Juvencus* manuscript. This is housed in Cambridge University Library as is the *Computus* Fragment, an astrological treatise dated c. 920 AD.

There is also a significant body of literature

composed in old Welsh which has survived in early medieval manuscripts. It is generally accepted that the verse saga known as *Y Gododdin* was composed originally in c.600 AD although its earliest survival in manuscript form dates from the thirteenth century. It is the tragic account of failed attacks by the men of Gododdin on an Anglian military camp at Catraeth (Catterick). The attacking force was annihilated, leaving perhaps one survivor, as well as the poet, Aneirin. The understated restraint of such lines as *'Ac wedi elwch tawelwch fu'*, (And after revelry there was silence), encapsulates the succinct beauty of this early Welsh verse.

A contemporary of Aneirin, the poet Taliesin, wrote a series of praise poems to Urien, king of Rheged c. 580 too, and these form part of the legacy of the writings of the *Cynfeirdd* (the early poets) in the Welsh language. They belong, rather ironically, not to the land of Wales itself, but to *Yr Hen Ogledd* (the Old North).

However, another cycle of poems written in Old Welsh can certainly be located in Wales. These poems are associated with the sagas of Llywarch Hen and Heledd c. 800 AD. They recount the tragic fate of the royal house of Powys, and, as Janet Davies notes, 'in their restrained passion, they are among the greatest glories of Welsh literature'.

'Y Gododdin' by artist Mary Lloyd Jones, who explores the long history of language in much of her work

The other Brittonic tongues:

Cornish: In 878 AD the kingdom of Cornwall fell to the Saxons, but the native language survived until the eighteenth century, when the last known speaker, Dolly Pentraeth, died. Today ardent Cornish nationalists are trying to revive the ancient language and its culture.

Cumbric: The Cumbric-speaking kingdoms of southern Scotland and north-west England had collapsed by the eleventh century; but certain place-names such as Penrith and Lanark (*llannerch* in Welsh, meaning 'grove') are reminders of early Brittonic origins, as was the system of counting sheep found among shepherds in this area until fairly recently.

Breton: Spoken in Brittany by c. 300,000 speakers today. Until the twelfth century it was the language of the nobility in this part of France, but during the last centuries it has been cast as an unofficial language and treated as an inferior *patois*. In 1977 *Diwan* schools were established to teach Breton by immersion, but attempts at incorporating them into the state education system have failed. Others have campaigned for more Breton programmes on the media, and for use of the language on road signs. This has had very limited success, but in 2008 the French did recognise Breton as a language within the country. At present, Breton is an endangered language.

Welsh in the Middle Ages

Lord Rhys ap Gruffudd, Prince of Deheubarth

On the eve of the Norman conquest of Wales, most of the country's population and, indeed, that of the neighbouring lands west of Offa's Dyke spoke Welsh as an everyday language. It had survived sporadic Viking raids almost unscathed, but the Norman invasions provided a sterner challenge. In England, the English tongue succumbed to Norman-French as the prestigious language of the royal court and high culture before its revival in the late thirteenth century. In Wales, Norman lords and English workers soon settled in the fertile coastlands of the Vale of Glamorgan, on the Gower peninsula, the north Wales coast, and the new borough towns, and as a result Welsh had to give way to French and English speech. In the hundreds of Rhos and Daugleddau, in what is Pembrokeshire today, King Henry 1st planted a Flemish colony, uprooting the native Welsh. Due to this influx of foreigners into the heartland of Wales, the giving and taking of hostages and the impact of war with Norman lords, many of the Welsh nobility were probably conversant with several languages at this time, and such personal names as Hywel Sais (the Englishman) and Elidir Sais seem to bear this out.

But in 'Pura Wallia' (pure Wales) under the leadership of native princes, and later the nobility, most Welsh people were monolingual. On his journey through Wales, preaching to attract soldiers to join the Third Crusade in 1188, Gerald of Wales notes that they had to employ the services of an interpreter, Alexander Cuhelyn, the archdeacon of Bangor, to translate from Norman French and Latin into Welsh.

During this period Welsh literature flourished and prospered greatly, producing some of the finest poetry and prose in its history. The first ever *eisteddfod* (although this name was not actually used for it) was held by Lord Rhys ap Gruffudd to celebrate Christmas at his new stone castle at Cardigan in 1176. One of Rhys's own harpists was the victorious musician, while a poet from north Wales won the coveted bardic chair. He was probably one of the poets of the independent Welsh princes (1100-1282), *Y Gogynfeirdd* (the fairly early poets); highly revered professional craftsmen whose intricately woven verses are formulaic expressions of praise to their patrons or else elegies on their death.

After the fall of the house of Gwynedd in the 1280s, the nobility took over responsibility for the patronage of the 150 or so bards of late medieval Wales. Hundreds of thousands of lines of poetry

Artist Margaret Jones has specialised in paintings of the Mabinogion – collated here on one map, showing the location of particular events in the legends

have survived, 'an almost industrial level of versification', for a small and not very wealthy country. The poems reflect all aspects of medieval life and are composed in strict metre or *cynghanedd,* which demands an incredible command of the Welsh language and which, at its best, can sustain works of great beauty.

Prose literature also reached great heights in the Middle Ages. Although the collection of eleven prose tales called the Mabinogion recall ancient Celtic gods, beliefs and customs, and might have been orally transmitted by professional storytellers or *cyfarwyddiaid* for centuries, they were written down between 1050 and 1170. These tales, especially *Culhwch ac Olwen* and the Four Branches of the Mabinogi, continue to delight readers today with their wit and style and they have been reproduced orally, as literary texts and in cartoons many times.

In medieval times the Welsh language also developed as a legal language. The early native Welsh laws are usually associated with the reign of King Hywel Dda (the Good) c. 940 AD, but once more the manuscript texts which have survived were written down from 1250 onwards, and contain both earlier and contemporary laws. These laws were just, community laws and the vast number of legal terms embodied in them prove that the Welsh-language was a practical, useful, competent and sophisticated language for governance during the early Middle Ages. The Welsh law texts, for their clarity of style and content, have justifiably been considered one of the most splendid creations of Welsh language culture.

Further evidence of the practical value of the Welsh language in the early Middle Ages can be found in the historical chronicles, for example, *Brut y Tywysogion* – the Chronicle of the Princes, which record the main events of Welsh history in chronological order. The surviving manuscripts are translations of a Latin original undertaken by Cistercian monks. Most of the text is concise and unadorned but at times it waxes eloquent and conveys momentous and lesser occasions in the history of Wales with great empathy, conviction and verve.

Spoken Welsh at this time could boast a number of dialects. In his *Description of Wales,* in 1194, Gerald of Wales comments upon the relative merits (in his opinion) of the main ones:

> *It is thought that the Welsh language is richer, more carefully pronounced and preferable in all respects in North Wales, for the area has far fewer foreigners. Others maintain that the speech of Cardiganshire in South Wales is better articulated and more to be admired, since it is in the middle and the heartland of Wales.*

Many English and Norman French words were assimilated into Welsh during medieval times; among them would be *barwn* (baron) and *cwrsi* (kerchief) from Norman French and from English *bwa* (bow) and *dug* (duke).

Dafydd ap Gwilym (fl. c.1330-50) is readily acknowledged to be the finest Welsh poet of all time and among the best in Europe. His poems, often about love and the world of nature, illustrate the richness and vitality of the Welsh language in the Middle Ages. In this extract he describes arriving at a country tavern and taking a fancy to a young girl:

Hywel Dda, King of all Wales c. 940

I come to a choice town
followed by my handsome page-boy...
I was a proud young man
and I had some wine...
I spotted a fair slender maid
in the house, my one fair sweetheart...
I made an agreement (love was not idle)
to come to the lovely girl
when the crowds had gone
to sleep; she was a dark-browed beauty.

(from *Trafferth mewn Tafarn* /
Trouble in a Tavern)

Above: *page from Peniarth 28 manuscript of the Welsh Laws*

Below: *a modern interpretation of the Laws of Women by the artist Peter Lord at the Hywel Dda Heritage Centre, Whitland*

Gradually, in the late Middle Ages, and in spite of the language's capacity to adapt to all aspects of life, English law began to replace the old Welsh laws and the language began to be considered as a slightly inferior medium in administration and in the church. During the major revolt of Owain Glyndŵr (1400-15) an attempt was made to stem this trend. The Pennal Policy of 1406, which laid out some of the policies for an independent Welsh state, demanded that all the clergy in Wales (who also served as clerks) should know the Welsh language.

The Act of Union and all that!

If the people of Wales rejoiced when one of their own, Henry VII or Henry Tudor, was crowned King of England and Wales in 1485, the dawn of the Tudor era brought mixed blessings for the Welsh language. The gentry increasingly turned their eyes towards the Tudor court in London for honours and promotion, and the bond between the native poets and their stalwart patrons began to loosen. Within a century, there were few professional bards left, and the language became the domain of the lesser gentry, the craftspeople and the *gwerin*, or ordinary people. To 'get on in the world' many Welsh people adopted English ways, especially in their surnames. The custom in Welsh had been to call someone after his father's name, thus Rhodri ap Huw (Rhodri son of Huw), or by some physical distinguishing mark, as in Dafydd Foel (the bald). But during the sixteenth century this practice went out of fashion and surnames became increasingly anglicised.

The Act of Union as depicted in The National Pageant of Wales, Cardiff, 1909

The humanist grammarian, Gruffydd Robert mocked the new subservient attitudes of Tudor Wales towards its native language. In 1567 he wrote from the safety of religious exile in Milan:

> '. . . Because you have some who, as soon as they see the river Severn, or the belfries of Shrewsbury, and hear an Englishman say "good morrow", they begin to forget their Welsh, and they speak in a shoddy language . . . and thus I urge every natural Welshman to pay his due debt of love to the Welsh language.'

Severn Crossing linking Wales and England

All these trends towards following English fashion found further expression in one clause in the Act of Union of 1536, passed during the reign of Henry VIII. This Act gave the Welsh people the right to enjoy the same privileges under English law as their counterparts in England 'as a very Member and joint of the same'. In order to ensure uniformity within the realm, it was also deemed necessary to abolish 'all and singular the sinister Usuages and Customs differing from the same . . .'. Thus all law courts were to conduct their proceedings in the English tongue and all court officers had to be fluent in English to enact this legislation effectively.

In this way, without argument or discussion even, the hated 'language clause' was passed by the English parliament. Neither the king nor Thomas Cromwell, the act's architect, probably intended the clause as a means of obliterating the Welsh language. The aim was merely to ensure uniformity and stability, to enable the passing of laws which would enforce the acceptance of the Protestant Reformation. But the clause's impact was much more significant and far-reaching. The Welsh language no longer had official status in its own law-courts or in its own country; as historian Gwyn A. Williams so colourfully proclaimed, 'Welsh ceased to be an official language and had to retreat to the kitchen'; henceforth it would officially be a second class language. The history of the Welsh language after 1536 is largely a history of the struggle to reverse this position and to regain official status for the language. Different generations would interpret such a task in very different ways.

A Bible for all the People of the World

Translating the Scriptures into Welsh

Y BEIBL CYSSEGR-LAN. SEF
YR HEN DESTAMENT, A'R NEWYDD.

2. Timoth. 3. 14, 15.

Eithr aros di yn y pethau a ddyscaist, ac a ymddyriedwyd i ti, gan wybod gan bwy y dyscaist.
Ac i ti er yn fachgen wybod yr scrythur lân, yr hon sydd abl i'th wneuthur yn ddoeth i iechydwriaeth, trwy'r ffydd yr hon sydd yng-Hrist Iesu.

Imprinted at London by the Deputies of
CHRISTOPHER BARKER,
Printer to the Queenes most excellent Maiestie.

1588.

The reign of Henry VIII also signalled the fall of the Roman Catholic Church in England and Wales and the founding of Protestantism as the official religion. Now, services were conducted in the vernacular English, rather than in medieval Latin, and the Bible and the Book of Common Prayer were translated into English. But the Welsh people could not be assimilated into this new church as easily, for they could not understand the English services, while the Latin liturgy had at least been familiar. The church hierarchy began to fear rebellion and disunity. For these very reasons a small group of Protestant humanists lobbied Queen Elizabeth I and her parliament, arguing that it would be highly advantageous if the scriptures could be translated into Welsh, lest the people be 'utterly destitute of God's Holy Word . . . and remain in more Darkness and Ignorance than they were in the Time of Papistry'.

Thus, in 1563, 'The Act for the Translation of the Bible and the Divine Service into the Welsh Tongue' was passed by parliament and within four years the New Testament and the Book of Common Prayer had been completed. The act also stipulated that another aim would be to place the new Welsh version of the Bible side by side with the English version in parish churches throughout Wales, so that the Welsh people could compare the texts and learn English more quickly.

The instigators of the Act and the main translators were William Salesbury and Bishop Richard Davies of St David's. Unfortunately, however, in spite of being the greatest Welsh scholar of his generation, and the one to fully realise the importance of securing 'the scriptures in your language', William Salesbury's translation was idiosyncratic and difficult to read. According to tradition, Davies and Salesbury, when working towards translating the rest of the Bible, quarrelled over the meaning of one word.

Stamps of 1988 commemorating the translation of the Bible into Welsh

The onerous task of completing the translation of the Bible was undertaken by William Morgan, Llanrhaeadr ym Mochnant. In English history the year 1588 is celebrated as the year when the Spanish Armada was defeated, but in Welsh history it also resonates significantly as it was the year William Morgan completed the Welsh version of the Bible and it was published. Morgan did lean heavily upon Salesbury's pioneering scholarship, but he was also a great scholar of Hebrew, Latin and Greek and steeped in the bardic tradition of Wales. His translation combined these elements and it was, as his fellow Protestant, Morris Kyffin, proclaimed in 1595 'a necessary task, masterly, godly and learned; for which the Welsh people will never be able to repay him with the thanks which he so deserves'.

And so, in the very century when the Welsh language had been declared an unofficial tongue, and when the magisterial medieval bardic tradition was waning, the crucial contribution of the Welsh humanists of the sixteenth century – writing, translating and publishing religious and other books in the Welsh language, cannot be over-emphasised or over-appreciated. The Welsh Bible of 1588, in particular, provided the nation with a splendid and pure standard of written Welsh which would form the basis of all literary activities for the next centuries, and help to prevent the language from fragmenting into a series of disconnected dialects.

Memorial to William Morgan at St Asaph

William Morgan

He saw that the Welsh language was only the common dialect
Of fair, farm, ballad and harp and tune;
And that the tongue which spoke in the markets of Monmouth
Could not understand the guttural speech of the markets of Anglesey.

. . . Let us praise him for his determination, his bravery and his holiness
And for his help in keeping the nation and the literary language alive,
Endowing it with the dignity and the highest honour
By turning it into one of the dialects of God's Revelation.

translated from the Welsh of D. Gwenallt Jones (1899-1969)

Preachers and Dreamers

A Sunday School banner from Trecynon, featuring 'The Good Shepherd'

Following the translation of the scriptures into Welsh, most Welsh people had become staunchly Protestant, and attendees of the Church of England. But there was a growing tide of nonconformity, signalled by the writings of martyr John Penry (d.1593) from Breconshire. Although he advocated the use of English, he also realised that it was impractical to convert a monolingual people to any religion without speaking to them in their native tongue.

This attitude set the tone for the growth of such Nonconformist sects as the Baptists and Independents. Both were English in origin, but in Wales their adherents acknowledged the significance of the Welsh language in the battle to save Welsh souls. Likewise, the great leaders and preachers of the Methodist revival of the eighteenth century, Howell Harris and Daniel Rowland, sought their converts through the Welsh language. Through their fiery and engaging sermons they introduced a common, standardised form of spoken pulpit Welsh, which transcended local dialects and which ensured that the brilliant prose of the Bible became part of their adherents' heritage. The beautiful hymns of William Williams, Pantycelyn, crystallised the teaching of the Methodists and ultimately became icons of the Welsh language.

The early educational trusts were fired by a similar motive to save souls. They established their voluntary schools to teach the Welsh people to read the scriptures. But they failed to recognise that such an aim could not succeed unless conducted through the medium of Welsh. In this respect, the circulating schools of Anglican minister, Griffith Jones of Llanddowror, Carmarthenshire, were fundamentally different. Men, women and children of all ages were encouraged to attend the temporary schools to learn to read the scriptures – but this time in Welsh. It was claimed

that by 1760 the movement had taught 160,000 children and c. 300,000 adults to read. Although this claim is perhaps exaggerated, it is probably true that by the end of the eighteenth century most adults in Wales were literate in Welsh – a truly formidable achievement which attracted the admiration of Catherine the Great of Russia. The Sunday school movement which went from strength to strength during the nineteenth century continued this astonishing feat and maintained a high level of literacy in the Welsh language.

While the language flourished as the medium of religious worship and devotion, as a literary medium it had become more and more the provenance of the *gwerin* (the common folk), who produced ballads, interludes, almanacs and *penillion* (verses) aplenty in Welsh.

It was not until the mid-eighteenth century that there was a revival in the classical bardic tradition. With it grew a desire to revive and reform the eisteddfodau, which had fallen into disrepute as unregulated and rowdy tavern competitions. The London-Welsh based Gwyneddigion society decided to sponsor what is now considered to be the first modern eisteddfod, organised by Thomas Jones in Corwen in 1789. Three years later, Edward Williams, or Iolo Morgannwg, the great forger and exotic genius, founded and held his fantastical druidic ceremony, the Gorsedd of the Bards, at Primrose Hill in London. Although the whole event was based upon a falsehood, nurtured in Iolo's fertile imagination, when it was linked to the eisteddfod at Carmarthen in 1819, it succeeded in providing the Welsh people with much-needed Welsh-language ceremonial and a unique and colourful national institution. It was to prove a jewel in the culture through challenging and difficult times ahead.

Hen benillion/Old rhymes

This is what I read – that each
Land's language has eight parts of speech;
Seems the women grabbed – God bless 'em –
Seven parts of the eight between them.

My sweetheart this year is like wind before rain –
He loves far and near, but what does he gain?
Those constant of heart they love truly but one,
And he who loves many ends up having none.

translated from the Welsh

The Gorsedd of the Bards, invented by Iolo Morganwg, but still flourishing in the twenty-first century

The Industrial Revolution and its Impact

Dowlais Ironworks by George Childs

The nineteenth century proved to be critical for the Welsh language. At its beginning the majority of the people of Wales spoke the language in their everyday lives, while half a million people were probably monoglot speakers. It was a period of great population growth and from decade to decade the absolute numbers of Welsh speakers probably increased significantly. It was also a period of population shift. The inexorable progress of the industrial revolution, especially in iron-working, drew droves of rural workers to seek better lives in south-east Wales. A town such as Merthyr Tydfil, the largest in Wales in 1830, with a population of 30,000, would have been home to a vibrant Welsh-speaking population. The expanding population allowed the language to become an urban and industrialised tongue. In this way the Welsh colonised their own country and did not have to emigrate to seek employment and stability, although many did seek 'the good life' in North America and later in Australia. This is in stark contrast to the fate of the Irish language, which suffered huge losses of speakers through the deaths and wholesale emigration following the Great Famine of 1845.

The middle of the century was a very fertile period for the printing press in Wales. Each religious denomination supported at least one Welsh-language monthly periodical and the newspaper, *Baner ac Amserau Cymru,* first printed in 1859, could claim a twice-weekly readership of 50,000.

Welsh culture found some new patrons among the gentry. In Gwent, Augusta Hall, Lady Llanofer, avidly promoted the eisteddfodic tradition and Lady Charlotte Guest of Cyfarthfa Castle, with the help of the Welsh scholar, Carnhuanawc, presented an English translation of the classics, *The Mabinogion*, to a wider public.

Augusta Hall

Meanwhile, father and son, Evan and James James of Pontypridd composed a patriotic song in 1856 which would become the National Anthem of Wales, *Hen Wlad fy Nhadau*. The last line of this fine anthem, '*O bydded i'r hen iaith barhau*' (Oh may the old language endure) foresaw, perhaps, the difficult days ahead for the ancient, native tongue.

This were also a period of social and economic unrest in Wales; from the Merthyr Rising of 1831; the Chartist revolt in Newport in 1839 to the uprising of the rural Rebecca Rioters in 1839-43. One constant grievance aired by the rioters was the gap which existed between the English-speaking iron and coal masters, landlords and magistrates on the one hand and the majority Welsh-speaking workers and their families on the other. This difference in language could hinder the administration of justice. Cases were tried in a language barely understood by the defendants and the provision of court interpreters was haphazard. No doubt, too, Welsh would have been used for plotting such disturbances, so that the authorities felt justified in regarding the Welsh language as conducive to riot and subversion. This attitude was to have serious repercussions in the years to come.

Top and centre: the National Anthem celebrated in art and craft
Below: sculpture in honour of the composers, in Pontypridd

Hen Wlad Fy Nhadau

Mae hen wlad fy nhadau yn annwyl i mi,
Gwlad beirdd a chantorion, enwogion o fri;
Ei gwrol ryfelwyr, gwladgarwyr tra mâd,
Dros ryddid collasant eu gwaed.

(Cytgan)
Gwlad, gwlad, pleidiol wyf i'm gwlad.
Tra môr yn fur i'r bur hoff bau,
O bydded i'r hen iaith barhau.

The land of my fathers is dear to me,
Old land where the minstrels are honoured and free;
Its warring defenders so gallant and brave,
For freedom their life's blood they gave.

(Chorus)
Country, country, true am I to my country,
While seas secure the land so pure,
O may the old language endure.

The Treason of the Blue Books and its Consequences

In 1846, the Llanpumpsaint born M.P. for Coventry, William Williams, called for the government to inquire into the state of education in Wales, and 'especially into the means afforded to the labouring classes for obtaining knowledge of the English language'. Thus, a commission was established and three vigorous but inexperienced, Anglican, English barristers, Lingen, Symons and Vaughan-Johnson, were appointed to gather evidence and produce the report. They, in turn, depended upon Anglican clergy and the lower gentry as clerks and witnesses.

In educational terms they fulfilled their brief satisfactorily, drawing attention not only to the gross inadequacies of 'school' buildings and resources, run mainly by the National and British societies and by private enterprises, but also to the teachers' lack of training and knowledge. They praised some of the schools they visited, and were particularly complimentary towards the standards achieved by Sunday Schools in general.

Unfortunately, however, the commissioners went far beyond their original brief, for they chose to make moral judgments on a people whom they could not possibly understand and on a way of life they could barely comprehend. They criticized Welsh women for what they perceived to be their lack of chastity and their slovenly nature and the Nonconformists for succouring such immorality.

They also insinuated that the Welsh language was the root of all this evil. They castigated the schoolmasters and mistresses for their lack of mastery in English and made several depreciative comments about the value and status of the native language.

A few examples will suffice:

Regarding Thomas Jones, schoolmaster of Cilcain, Flintshire:

'His knowledge of English is so limited that I was frequently obliged to interpret my questions into English…'

'My district exhibits the phenomenon of a peculiar language isolating the mass from the upper portion of society . . . his language keeps him under the hatches (in his new industrial home) . . . It is the language of old-fashioned agriculture, of theology, and of simple rustic life, while all the world about him is English . . .'

Welsh, then, was considered an adequate and suitable language for the hearth and for religious meetings, but without doubt 'to get on in the world' one would need to be fluent in English. Many (among them notable Anglican clergy) hastened to refute the report's conclusions, and by 1854 it had been dubbed 'The Treason of the Blue Books'.

But many also felt a deep shame at its findings. In the field of morality the Welsh people strove to prove that they were as respectable and unadulterated as their self-righteous neighbours. In educational terms the report had far-reaching and very negative effects. The claim made in it that 'you could not find in the most purely Welsh parts, a single parent . . . who would not have his child taught English in school' was probably true; this was, after all, the age of the rapid growth of the British Empire, when English was being imposed on all its other colonies world-wide. Its nearest neighbour, Wales, had little hope to promote its language against the leviathan presence on its doorstep. This attitude mirrored the opinion of the editor of *The Times*, in 1866, who saw the Welsh language as 'the curse of Wales', a barrier to intellectual and economic progress. Tragically, at this crucial stage in the nation's linguistic development no one thought that this would have been a golden opportunity to champion the advantages of a bilingual education.

In 1861, a 'Revised Code' introduced financial rewards for schools if they could show inspectors that the pupils were making good progress in reading and writing English. This, and the Education Act of 1870, led to elementary education throughout Wales becoming more and more English in content and ethos and the Welsh language was marginalised.

An extract from the Tywyn British School log-book, Friday 13, 1863 reads:

> 'I feel at a loss to know the best method, to adopt in order to prevent the children generally from speaking Welsh. Today, I have introduced a 'Welsh Stick' into each of the Classes, and the child who has it last is to be kept in half an hour after School hours.'

Three million bilingual speakers . . .

'The Society for the Utilisation of the Welsh Language' was established in 1885 by Dan Isaac Davies, inspector of schools in Glamorganshire. His aim – the production of three million bilingual speakers by 1985 – was sincere, although Welsh was to be introduced into the elementary curriculum in order, primarily, to improve pupils' grasp of English. The instigator died soon afterwards and the society petered out.

The report of 1847 had also mentioned, but had not condoned, the use of the 'Welsh Not' or 'Stick' as a means of punishing errant pupils who persisted in using their native tongue. During the second half of the nineteenth century it was certainly a feature of several schools in west Wales in particular. It comprised a piece of wood carved with W.N. (or Welsh Not) which would be passed from one pupil heard speaking Welsh to another. At the end of the day or week the pupil wearing the tally-stick would be punished by caning. Similar versions were used in Ireland, Brittany and Kenya to discourage the use of the native language in schools. It encouraged children to spy on one another and taught them to consider their own language as inferior and second class.

The stigma of the Welsh Not certainly influenced O.M. Edwards of Llanuwchllyn, Merionethshire. He writes with passion of his hatred of it and therefore, when he became Chief Inspector of Schools in 1907, he ensured that teaching Welsh and through the medium of Welsh was encouraged and became the norm in elementary schools in Welsh-speaking areas.

Above: O.M. Edwards, pioneer of Welsh education
Below: Protest at the Welsh Office in Cardiff, 1983, part of the campaign for Welsh-medium education

While many Welsh people believed the accusations of the Blue Books, some patriots decided to emigrate to establish a Welsh-speaking colony abroad. Many moved to North America, but soon found that it was very difficult to keep their national identity intact in their new home. Thus, in 1865, due to the persuasion and determination of Michael D. Jones of Y Bala, 163 people sailed to Patagonia in Argentina to seek to establish a self-governing colony, which would run all its affairs through the Welsh language. The children of Patagonia, therefore, received a full Welsh-medium education in the nineteenth century. In spite of incredible privation, the colony, *Y Wladfa,* succeeded, but the language gradually lost ground to the official Argentinian Spanish. During recent years there has been a revival of interest, with young Patagonians visiting Wales to follow intensive Welsh classes, and language courses being organised in Cwm Hyfryd and Chubut in Patagonia.

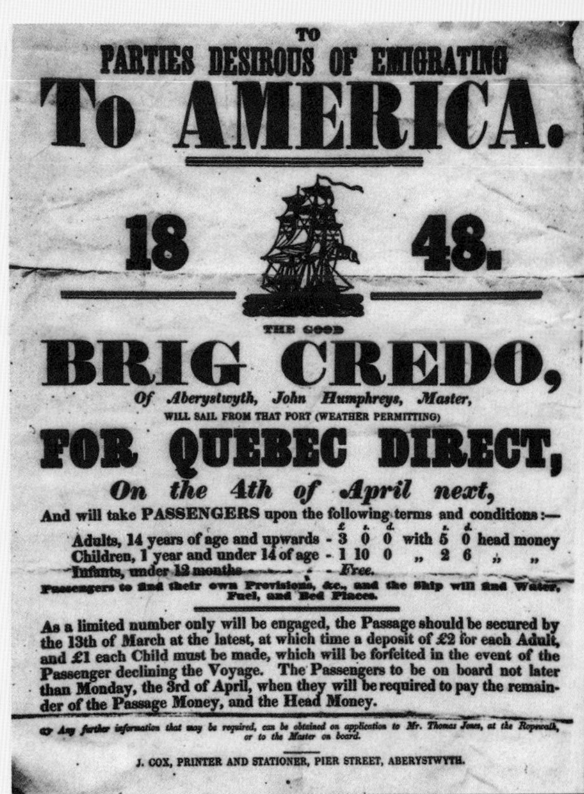

Top: an expedition from Aberystwyth to North America
Centre: The Mimosa, bound for Patagonia
Below: setting out for chapel, Y Gaiman, Patagonia

Coal miners, of whom an increasing number were incomers

Fluctuating Fortunes

The fortunes of the Welsh language fluctuated greatly during the last decades of the nineteenth century. Once more there was a significant growth in population and thus in the numbers of Welsh-speakers. But the incredible development of the coal industry with its huge demand for manual workers could no longer be satisfied from the pool of Welsh-speaking labourers from the countryside. The door opened to mass in-migration, mainly from the neighbouring counties of south-west England. These in turn often married Welsh girls, the language of the household became English and in the next generation Welsh was often cast to one side.

During this period Welsh-speakers went from being the majority of the population of Wales to a minority, although the actual numbers increased. For the first time, the 1891 Census asked people to record whether they could speak Welsh, English or both. 910,289 or 56% of the population claimed to be Welsh-speaking. By 1901 the numbers had increased to 929,824 but the percentage had fallen to 49.9%. This trend continued up to 1911 when the highest number of Welsh speakers was recorded at 977,366 but this constituted a percentage of only 43.5% - a significant decrease over all.

David Lloyd George, a Welsh-speaking Prime Minister

Until this period the language had always been considered an essential element in defining Welsh identity. Now, many people living in Wales could claim no affinity with the native tongue but did feel that they belonged in their new home. Some of these became totally disaffected with the language; some were apathetic towards it and some felt threatened by its continued presence, and began to consider it as a divisive force in Welsh society.

The Welsh language did not have many friends in high places either, although it was the first language of maverick M.P. and later Prime Minister, Lloyd George – and he was proud of it. But there was considerable support for the setting up of national Welsh institutions, such as the founding of the University of Wales in 1893 from the constituent colleges of Aberystwyth (1872), Bangor (1884) Cardiff (1883) and Lampeter (1822). Each institution promoted the academic study of the Welsh language and its literature, although, bizarrely, the actual teaching was in English, and there were no subjects taught through the medium of Welsh. However, this academic study was a decisive step forward for the language, for it gave it intellectual status and prestige. It should also be remembered that, as Janet Davies states, 'students and graduates of Welsh have provided the shock troops of Welsh-language movements' during the twentieth century.

In 1907 the National Library of Wales was established at Aberystwyth. Its main responsibility is to collect and keep manuscripts, books and pictures relating to Wales or to the other Celtic countries.

This was also the period when confident Nonconformists were preoccupied by an almost pathological hatred of the Established Church. They argued that it was an alien church which had not, until 1870, appointed a single Welsh-speaking bishop for generations. This rather stilted interpretation of the church's attitude to the language, especially in view of the efforts of a group of literary clerics to promote Welsh literature and the eisteddfod, was compounded by Bishop Basil Jones of St David's ill-conceived comment in 1886, that Wales was no more than 'a geographical expression'. In 1920 the Church in Wales was disestablished and since then many of its bishops and clergy have contributed significantly to the enhanced position of Welsh in religious and secular life.

National Library of Wales, Aberystwyth

Emrys ab Iwan

At a time when British imperialism was at its height, Robert Ambrose Jones or Emrys ab Iwan of Abergele was a lone and independent thinker. He was an advocate for the Welsh-language when it was not fashionable at all:

> '. . . loosing our language would be a terrible loss. And without doubt we shall loose it sometime, unless we make more of an effort to keep it than we have so far . . . The Welsh people have nothing they can be especially proud of now, except the language; and yet! they, through great cost and effort are helping its detractors to abolish it. Oh! the unsavoury Vandalism . . . It is difficult to understand why Providence entrusted such a poetic and philosophical language to a people so many of whom are too dull to realise its worth.'

translated from the Welsh of Emrys ab Iwan (1851-1906)

New Challenges

Urdd members enjoy water sports

Challenges from outside Wales affected the course of the Welsh language in the early twentieth century. In the carnage of the First World War c. 20,000 young Welsh-speaking Welshmen were killed, depriving communities of a whole generation. Following the war the industrial base of Wales was decimated. The formerly economically successful Welsh-speaking slate-quarrying areas of north-west Wales went into irretrievable decline, and the steam-coalfield of the south Wales valleys shed workers, who had to brave unemployment or seek work in England. Rural Wales, still the heartland of the language, was also exposed to the depression. Between 1925 and 1939 about 390,000 Welsh people emigrated, never to return. Many began to question the point of speaking Welsh when their destiny seemed to be elsewhere. Socialists, except in the anthracite coal-mining valleys of the Gwendraeth, Tawe and Aman, came to regard the Welsh language and its accompanying nonconformist culture as old-fashioned and as obstructing social progress.

Statue of father and son O.M. Edwards and Ifan ab Owen Edwards in Llanuwchlyn

Considerable determination and self-confidence was required to swim against such a tide of negativity. This Sir Ifan ab Owen Edwards did by continuing his father's work as editor of the immensely popular Welsh-language magazine for children, *Cymru'r Plant,* and especially by founding the youth movement, *Urdd Gobaith Cymru (Fach)* in 1922. At the beginning, Urdd members were expected to swear allegiance to the language, buy and read Welsh books, sing Welsh songs and play through the medium of Welsh. Within a few years the membership was almost 25,000, reaching its zenith in 1940 with 57,000 members. The movement still attracts a membership of over 50,000 in 900 branches throughout Wales, and can be credited with inspiring generations of both

Welsh-speakers and learners to embrace the language and culture through its eisteddfodau, its modern activities and its residential centres at Glan-llyn and Llangrannog.

In the field of education, a report, *Y Gymraeg mewn Addysg a Bywyd* (The Welsh Language in Education and Life), chaired by the language supremo, W.J.Gruffydd, was published in 1927. The report was unstinting in its criticism of the lack of support for teaching Welsh, the inadequacies of the teacher training programmes and the poor resources for language teaching. With 'almost religious zeal' it recommended that Welsh should be taught to all the children of Wales, irrespective of geography or home background.

Gruffydd and fellow Cardiffians were also instrumental in taking on the anglicised world of broadcasting, and in 1937 the Welsh Region of the BBC was created. This development required the BBC to employ bilingual professional producers and presenters, who would succeed in evolving an accessible standard of spoken Welsh, which came to replace the formal pulpit Welsh which had served the nation well during the nineteenth century but which was now outmoded.

A further boost was given to the prestige of the Welsh language when the National Eisteddfod Court decided that Welsh should be the festival's only official language. This 'Welsh Rule', unpopular with certain anti-Welsh factions, was enacted for the first time at Caerffili in 1951. In the meantime Parliament had passed the Welsh Courts Act in 1942, which, by stating that Welsh could be used in court by any who might feel disadvantaged by not doing so, began the process of reversing the impact of the 'language clause' of the 1536 Act of Union.

Above: Radio broadcasting from Bangor, 1938
Below: the daily news programme Heddiw *from BBC studios in Cardiff, 1972*

Mynydd Epynt

The impact of the Second World War was not as dramatic for the language as the First. Many of the young evacuees from England were assimilated into the Welsh-speaking rural communities. But in one part of Wales the effect was devastating, as the War Office took the land of the Mynydd Epynt farmers in Breconshire, and turned it into a firing range, removing 400 Welsh-speakers from their community, and moving the boundary of Welsh-speaking Wales 15 kilometres westwards at one fell swoop.

The anguish of this dispersal was recorded by Iorwerth C. Peate:

> In Waun Lwyd . . . I went past the gable end of the house to the front. There I found an 82-year-old lady. I shall never forget her: she sat there like a statue staring at the moor land with tears flowing down her cheeks . . . 'My dear boy', she said, 'go back there (Cardiff) as soon as you can, it is the end of the world here.'

Campaigning for the Language

Protest by Cymdeithas yr Iaith Gymraeg, the Welsh language society, at Aberystwyth Post Office, 1963

The census figures cast a shadow over attempts at reviving the language during the second half of the twentieth century. In 1951 the number of speakers had fallen to 714,868, which was 28.9% of the population; in 1971, 542,425 or 20.9% claimed to be competent in Welsh and by 1991 there had been a further drop to 508,098 or 18.6%. Certain trends were also becoming more and more evident. By the 1960s, very few monolingual Welsh speakers remained; bilingualism was becoming the norm; and the concept of '*Y Fro Gymraeg*' (Welsh-speaking Wales), as a swathe of heartland extending from the north-west to the south-west, where daily life could be carried on wholly through the medium of Welsh, was rapidly eroding. A new linguistic landscape was being forged. Although only 13.3% of the population of the Rhondda valley could speak Welsh in 1971, they numbered 11,295 speakers – a third of the population of Welsh-speaking Merionethshire.

It is hardly surprising then that morale and the status of the Welsh language were at a low ebb during the 1950s. There was a general feeling of crisis but little idea of how to respond to it. And yet the seeds of the later revival were sown during this decade.

It was the greed of Liverpool corporation and other English conurbations for Welsh water that galvanised a sense of outrage among Welsh people throughout the country. The drowning of Cwm Tryweryn, near Y Bala, awoke a very strong reaction among almost all the local authorities and Welsh MPs and the drowned village of Cwm Celyn became a symbol of the political helplessness of the Welsh people. They had failed to defend a Welsh-speaking community from being annihilated.

In the meantime in industrial west Wales, Eileen and Trevor Beasley had begun their lonely but truly heroic campaign of civil disobedience by refusing to pay their rates to Llanelli Rural District Council until they were sent bilingual forms. Between 1952 and 1960 they appeared before the courts sixteen times and bailiffs seized goods from their home on six occasions,

Famous graffiti, 'Remember Tryweryn', at Llanrhystud

one time leaving only a pot of jam on an empty bookshelf.

The Beasleys' unwavering stand for their rights as Welsh speakers was the inspiration behind Saunders Lewis's radio lecture, *Tynged yr Iaith* (The Fate of the Language) broadcast on February 13, 1962. Lewis was Honorary President of Plaid Cymru (the Welsh nationalist party), but that did not prevent him from expressing the frustrations felt by many in its ranks, and especially amongst the young, that the party was more concerned with winning parliamentary seats than with the fate of the Welsh language. In his lecture, Lewis used the Beasleys' example to show how unconstitutional actions could bring about important changes. His gloomy prediction that unless such uncompromising, indeed revolutionary, action was taken immediately, the Welsh language would not survive into the twenty-first century. His main call was for the Welsh language to become an official language of local and national government in Wales. This should be Plaid Cymru's priority, 'for without the Welsh language any kind of self-government would be of little value to Wales'.

Saunders Lewis's lecture was the main stimulus for a group of young intellectuals, based mainly around Aberystwyth, to establish *Cymdeithas yr Iaith Gymraeg* (the Welsh language society) in the summer of 1962. It was to be a single-issue protest movement, dedicated to restoring the official status of the language, through unconstitutional means if necessary. Thus began a long and sustained campaign, conducted on many fronts, and employing many different tactics to attain this aim. The members emulated civil disobedience movements world wide, especially those of the peace movements and civil rights campaigns in the USA. Initially the emphasis was on securing Welsh language forms: court summons, vehicle licences and birth certificates. To draw attention to their

Above: Trevor and Eileen Beasley and family

Right: Saunders Lewis

Rali Glyndwr 2002
Rheoli'r Farchnad Dai

2pm - Medi 14
Neuadd Cyngor Ceredigion
Aberaeron
Meredydd Evans & Emyr Llywelyn

DEDDF EIDDO I GYMRU!

Rally for a Property Act for Wales

campaigns they sought to be arrested and brought before the courts. This led to the iconic but slightly comical sit-down protest on Trefechan Bridge in Aberystwyth in 1963 which brought a great deal of much-needed publicity to the cause. In 1967 a Welsh Language Act was passed, which went some of the way towards addressing some of the issues, but which also illustrated the need for far stronger legislation.

The society turned its attention next to the lack of Welsh on road signs, a campaign which was both highly popular with supporters and unpopular among other Welsh-speakers at the time. Initially they daubed the signs with green paint, and then removed them and delivered them to police stations. Other campaigns called for a Property Act and control of housing and second homes in Wales; positive local and central education policies; a Welsh-language television channel, and a more comprehensive Welsh Language Act.

Cymdeithas yr Iaith Gymraeg was, and is, primarily a young people / students' movement, with no more than 2,000 members at a time, but drawing upon the tacit and sometimes active support of mature, respectable, law-abiding sympathizers. Among the most influential of these in the early years was Alwyn D. Rees whose monthly editorials in the periodical *Barn* ensured that the authorities could not afford to ignore the youthful protests. During the many campaigns, hundreds of members and supporters were fined and around 200 were imprisoned. Since the mid-sixties the society had adopted a 'non-violence towards persons' policy as the cornerstone of its direct action campaigning. One important feature of the membership was the active involvement of young women. Among them were Meri Huws, Meg Ellis and Branwen Nicholas, who became chairpersons of the movement and served jail sentences for their convictions. As the campaigning evolved, it became more and more obvious that securing the linguistic rights of Welsh-speakers was not a sufficient goal. The emphasis had to shift to bolstering and securing the future of the Welsh-speaking communities themselves – in political, economic and social terms – and to urge the people of Wales themselves to embrace the language as their own. The achievements of *Cymdeithas yr Iaith Gymraeg* have been truly amazing and in many ways the Wales we know today would be a very different place but for the relentless, principled and often selfless actions of its members.

Dafydd Iwan and the road signs campaign

NOTEWORTHY PROTESTERS

Merched y Wawr

In 1966-7 members of the Women's Institute in Y Parc, a hamlet near Y Bala, rebelled against that movement's directive that all its official activities should be carried out in English. From this local protest a new national Welsh-medium movement for women, Merched y Wawr, evolved. Today it has about 280 branches and clubs throughout Wales, which organise over 2,250 social events and meetings through the medium of Welsh every year.

Angharad Thomas

As chair of *Cymdeithas yr Iaith Gymraeg* in the early eighties, Angharad Thomas was imprisoned several times. These jail sentences inspired her novel *Yma o Hyd* (Still Here) in which she reflects upon the responsibilities thrust upon her as a Welsh-speaker at such a crucial time in the language's history:

I'm afraid ... It's awful being afraid of the future, I'm not so afraid of seeing the demise of Wales as I am of having to live through the process. Because having to watch someone die is a dreadful experience. What a pity I wasn't born a generation earlier. What a pity I wasn't born a generation later. Any time but the present ...

translated extract from *Yma o Hyd*

Dafydd Iwan

Dafydd Iwan was *Cymdeithas yr Iaith Gymraeg*'s chairman during the society's most visual and perhaps controversial campaign – for bilingual road signs. He was also a popular singer who could fire the campaigns with his protest songs:

> We'll paint the world green, boys,
> Paint the world green;
> We'll fire up the Welsh, boys
> And paint the world green!

His satirical songs about the investiture of Charles as Prince of Wales in 1969 were particularly popular

GORAU ARF: THE BEST WEAPON

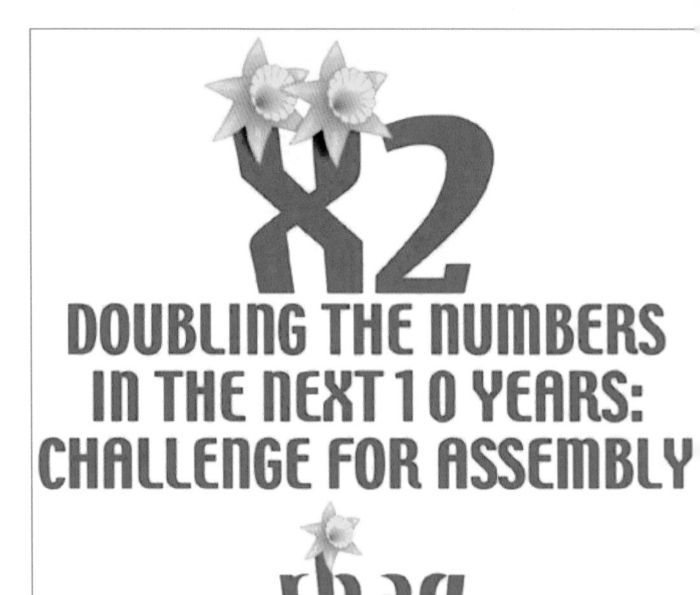

A challenge from parents: a ***rhag*** *poster*

There can be little doubt that developments in the field of education have been crucially important to the renewed vigour of the Welsh language in the last decades of the twentieth century. These developments have occurred at all levels, from nursery to higher education, and continue today.

Their roots go back to the Second World War when Sir Ifan ab Owen Edwards opened a private Welsh-medium primary school at Lluest, near Aberystwyth, under the auspices of Urdd Gobaith Cymru, to counteract the English-speaking influence of the evacuees, who flooded into the area in 1939-40. Although perhaps one could argue that this initiative removed the Welsh language from mainstream education in the area, it did serve to prove to sceptical Welsh-speaking parents that teaching through the medium of Welsh was not only practical but also educationally beneficial to the children.

After the war, in 1947, the first Welsh-medium primary school to be established by a local authority was opened at Ysgol Gymraeg (Dewi Sant), Llanelli. This was the first tentative step in a movement which has seen dramatic successes, as more and more parents demand a Welsh-medium education for their children. The early demand came mainly from the anglicised urban areas of the south- and north-east, initially led by Welsh-speaking middle-class speakers under the banner of Undeb Rhieni Ysgolion Cymraeg (Union of Parents of Welsh-medium Schools), since 1983 called Rhieni dros Addysg Gymraeg (Parents for Welsh-medium education). They were very concerned at the lack of teaching of, and through, the mother tongue in these areas. Gradually non-Welsh-speaking parents have become more and more involved; creating a demand for Welsh-medium schools which far out-strips current provision even today.

The first Welsh-medium secondary school was Ysgol Glanclwyd, Denbighshire, founded in 1956. Today, there are 24 such schools throughout Wales,

and the traditional Welsh-medium / bilingual primary and secondary schools in Welsh-speaking areas in Gwynedd and south-west Wales continue to extend and develop their Welsh-medium provision.

Welsh-medium nursery schools, founded in the fifties and sixties through voluntary efforts, came into existence initially to feed the new Welsh-medium primary schools. But the dire 1971 Census figure which noted that only 9,748 3-4-year-old children could speak Welsh throughout Wales shook the volunteers into a more strategic approach. In 1971 the national Welsh-medium nursery association, Mudiad Ysgolion Meithrin, was founded to lobby for more provision. Within a quarter of a century the movement could claim to have 13,900 members in a network of 645 *cylchoedd meithrin* (playgroups) and 407 *cylchoedd Ti a Fi* (parents' and toddlers' groups). Further challenges, especially the implications of the Children's Act and the new Foundation Phase in education with its strong emphasis on the validity of play and bilingualism, have influenced the movement greatly. With a state-of-the-art Integrated Centre and Headquarters in Aberystwyth and similar centres across Wales, Mudiad Ysgolion Meithrin's achievements have proved an inspiration to similar movements promoting nursery provision in lesser-used languages throughout the world.

At the other end of the spectrum the developments have been less dramatic. Only 3% of the students in higher education in Welsh universities received Welsh-medium teaching in 2004. This has led to vociferous and continuing campaigning, especially at Aberystwyth and Bangor, and has produced some results. The target has been set to raise this percentage to 7% by 2010.

The success of Welsh-medium education is well illustrated in the capital city itself. The original Welsh-medium school in Cardiff, Bryntâf, (established in 1949), was sub-divided into 4 schools in 1981, but they, in turn, have spawned 10 Welsh-medium primary schools, 3-4 starter classes and two secondary schools in the city, with others in the pipeline.

In 2008 Newport and Wrexham Councils organised surveys to assess the demand for Welsh-medium education. In Newport 31% of the parents said they would send their child to a Welsh-medium school if it was within a convenient distance to their home, and in Wrexham 69% felt that their children would benefit from Welsh-medium education.

It would seem then that for Welsh parents, the proverb *Gorau Arf, Arf Dysg* (The best weapon is the weapon of education) certainly rings true.

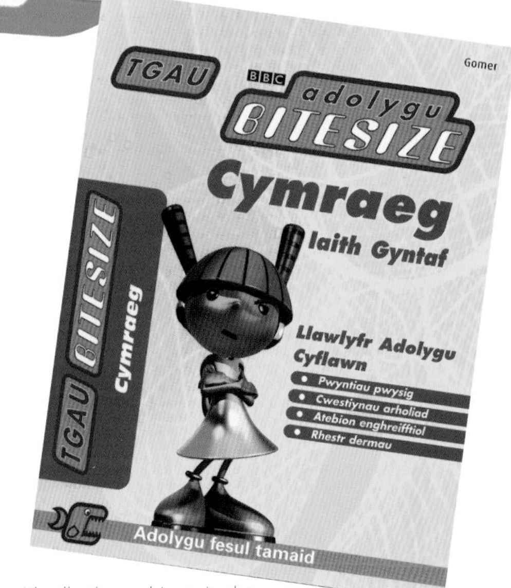

As with all other subjects in the curriculum, there is a revision guide for Welsh

Madison Tazu, Welsh Learner of the Year 2008

Cultural Life

Some of the more exciting developments during the last decades belong to the field of Welsh-language culture. Hundreds of Welsh books are published annually, mostly with the backing of the Welsh Books Council, founded in 1961. The best-sellers tend to be colourful books for the younger age group and the autobiographies of Welsh celebrities. Linked to these are the area newspapers, *papurau bro,* published monthly through the unstinting efforts of volunteers. Sixty-three separate titles are listed in 2009. This activity contributes to the industry of 42 printers and publishers, who work at least partly through the medium of Welsh, located throughout Wales. Attempts at founding a daily Welsh-language newspaper floundered in 2008, as it was deemed that a web-based publication would be more feasible. Certainly it is encouraging to see that the language has a considerable presence on the World Wide Web and that it has embraced the new technologies enthusiastically. Facebook has declared the Welsh language to be one to which material can be translated on its site.

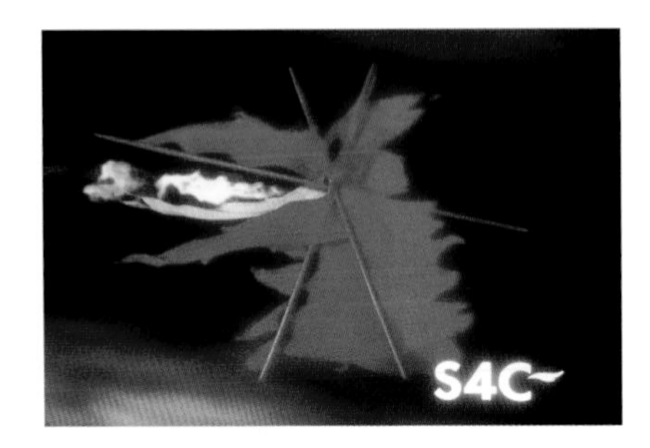

Another crucially significant aspect in the process of normalising the language in the modern world has been the development of BBC Radio Cymru (1977) and, on television, Sianel Pedwar Cymru, S4C (1982). Both these media bring the language into the home – still the most important of all the domains of the Welsh language. S4C was established following an arduous campaign by Cymdeithas yr Iaith and its supporters throughout the 1970s, and was brought to a head when the Honorary President of Plaid Cymru, Gwynfor Evans, threatened to starve to death unless the Conservative government of Margaret Thatcher honoured its pre-1979-election promise that the fourth television channel would be dedicated to Welsh-language programmes. The timely intervention of three elder statesmen averted a possible crisis, and in November 1982 the new channel, S4C, was launched.

Both media have a difficult brief to deliver as they have to please a very wide audience base. Among the more successful programmes have been those in the fields of news coverage and current affairs, sport, children's programmes, the longest serving soap opera on British television, *Pobol y Cwm*, and cutting-edge drama, such as the series *Con Passionate*.

Quintessentially Welsh, the National Eisteddfod remains one of Wales and Europe's strongest cultural traditions. Today, it provides a stage not only for the nation's best musicians, reciters, poets and prose writers but also as a forum for all kinds of fringe activities which promote the Welsh language. The variety of pavilions and stalls testify to a vibrant festival, where all-comers are welcome to taste and enjoy Welsh culture. Welsh-learners can touch base in *Maes D* (Learners' unit) while the young come out at night to partake of the music and revelry of *Maes B*. The National Eisteddfod's peripatetic itinerary ensures that it can help to boost the language's profile in the different areas it visits from year to year.

Wenglish

During the period of partial bilingualism several Welsh words found their way into the English language dialect of south Wales:

cawl: broth
cariad: love
ach-y-fi!: Ugh!
didoreth: slovenly in household matters
(h)anes: story / tale
wit wat (chwit chwat): unreliable.

D for *Dysgwr* (Welsh Learner)

A contributing factor in the language's new-found vitality must be the development of Welsh learners' courses. During the second half of the twentieth century there has been a steep rise in the in-migration of English speakers, particularly into the rural heartlands. Some of these immigrants do attend classes and master the new language. But the majority of learners come from among the non-Welsh-speakers of Wales itself, who wish to support their children's Welsh-medium education and who feel deprived of one part of their own birthright. In the 1970s intensive Wlpan courses, based upon the Hebrew model, were introduced and gradually the teaching methodologies have been honed and made more professional. One outstanding venture was the development in the 1980s of the Nant Gwrtheyrn Language Centre in a derelict mining village on the Llŷn Peninsula, as a residential Welsh learners' centre.

Every year, the accolade of 'Learner of the Year', is awarded during the National Eisteddfod. In 2008, Madison Tazu from Cardigan scooped this prestigious prize. As a school pupil she had rejected the language but on her later travels around the world she became ashamed of her lack of fluency in her own tongue. She returned to Wales and learned the language anew – with spectacular results!

Nia Parri, tutor at Maes D at the National Eisteddfod

Nant Gwrtheyrn language centre

Iaith Pawb – Everyone's Language

During the last decade of the twentieth century some optimistic politicians began to say that the battle to save the Welsh language had been won and that everyone could relax at last. Such optimism stemmed in part from the passing of a second Welsh Language Act in 1993, which gave statutory status to *Bwrdd yr Iaith Gymraeg*: the Welsh Language Board, and in which all public bodies were instructed to produce and activate language plans. It was felt that this would give the language equal status with English in all public services. Others argued that the legislation did not go far enough and the call for a stronger language act continues.

The Welsh Language Board fully recognised the importance of maintaining and sustaining the language as a vibrant community language. It acknowledged the significant contribution already made, since 1991, in this respect by Menter Cwm Gwendraeth – a venture set up to create social networks for the language to be used in everyday life in this Welsh-speaking area of Carmarthenshire. Nowadays there is a network of 21 such language ventures the length and breadth of Wales, sponsored by the Board, led mainly by young, dedicated and enthusiastic professionals.

Without doubt the establishment of the Welsh Assembly Government in 1998 has wrought a sea-change in attitudes towards the Welsh language within Wales and beyond. The Assembly has a full bilingual policy and the excellent translation services have made bilingual meetings acceptable and almost the norm. This has contributed to a new-found confidence in the language's ability to be relevant in all situations, both formal and informal. In 2003 the Assembly produced a seminal policy document – *Iaith Pawb: Everyone's Language* – which has formed the basis for all kinds of initiatives on behalf of the language. The aim of *Iaith Pawb* is 'to ensure that the Welsh language can be used freely in social, leisure and business activities throughout Wales and that the number of people in Wales able to speak Welsh continues to increase'. It is above all a policy document which calls upon all: ministers and officers, in local and

hapus i siarad
Cymraeg!

'Happy to speak Welsh': a Welsh Language Board Poster

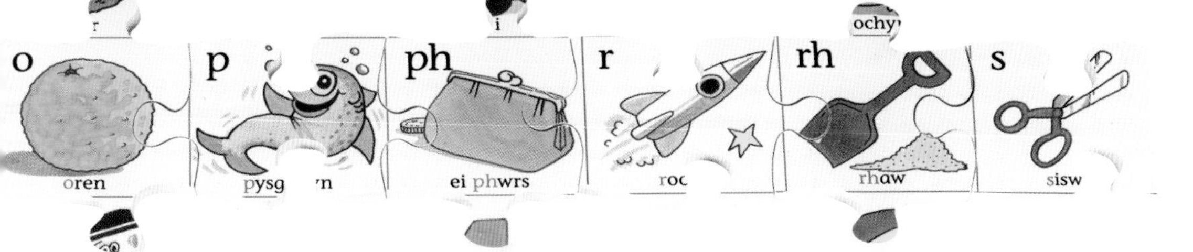

national government and even the public themselves to take responsibility for the Welsh language and to embrace its future as one of the two official languages of Wales. As the title so powerfully notes the Welsh language belongs to all the people of Wales – it is Everyone's Language.

The confidence inherent in *Iaith Pawb* was based partly on the latest 2001 census figures for Welsh speakers, which showed for the first time for almost a century, a small increase both in numbers and as a percentage of the Welsh population. The number of Welsh speakers (3 years old and over) was 575,730 and the percentage 20.5%. Furthermore, statisticians argued that around 28.43% had some measure of competency in the language. The most edifying aspect was that there was a distinctive upward trend among the 3-15 year old cohort, further proof that Welsh-medium education is a vital factor in the language's survival. The future of the language will be in their hands.

Enjoying Welsh at home

Twf (Growth)

One sobering feature of the 2001 census however was the decrease in the number of Welsh-speaking households and the lack of transmission of the language as a *mamiaith* (mother-tongue) on the hearth. J.A. Fishman's warning in his classic study, *Reversing the Language Shift,* 'Without intergenerational mother tongue transmission . . . no language maintenance is possible. That which is not transmitted cannot be maintained,' could not be ignored.

To address this issue the Welsh Language Board established the initiative, *Twf* (Growth), in the early twenty-first century. It aims at enlisting the support of midwives and health-visitors to discuss with young parents the advantages of raising their children bilingually – to show them that such an upbringing can bring social, cognitive, educational, cultural and economic advantages and blessings.

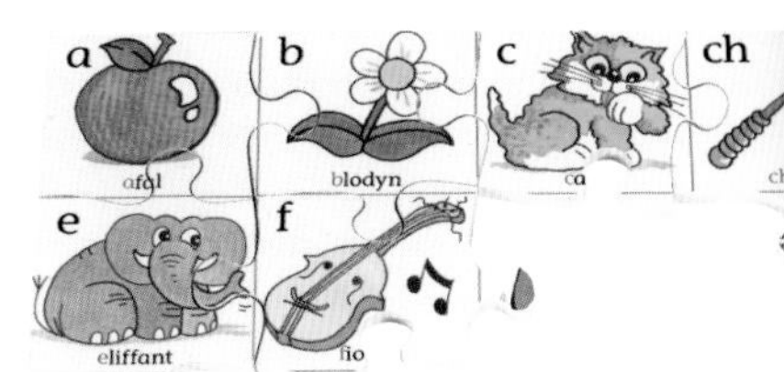

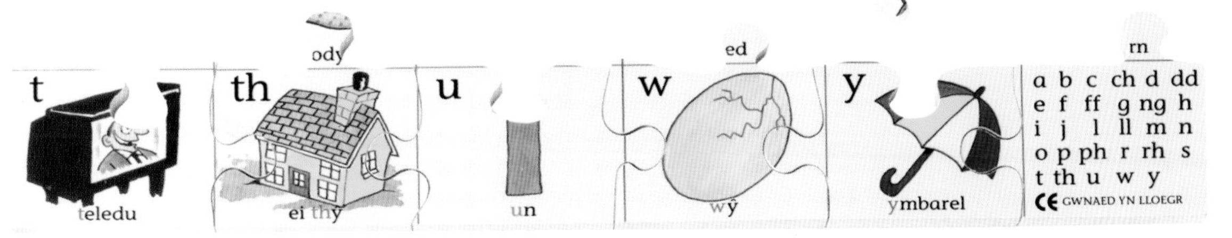

The Will to Survive

Only Men Aloud – proud winners of Last Choir Standing, 2008

How one regards the future of the Welsh language depends upon whether one is an optimist or a pessimist. There can be no doubt that the threats are still real. Among the most difficult challenges must be the increasing influence of the English language as the first truly international language. Its ascendancy threatens many other minority languages and cultures around the world. The future of merely half a million Welsh speakers is certainly at risk when there are 277 million English speakers between neighbouring England and America. Whatever the small comfort of the latest census figures, as the historians of the Welsh language, Aitchison and Carter, have warned, 'Triumphalism is not . . . in order; not yet, at least'. In view of all this, the amazing fact, perhaps, is that the Welsh language is *'yma o hyd'* (still here).

And yet there are so many very positive aspects. The language has been well-served by academics in recent years with the publication of a multi-volumed Welsh dictionary, the *tour de force* of *The Welsh Academy English-Welsh Dictionary* and the magisterial *Encyclopaedia of Welsh Life*. These are bolstered by on-line dictionaries and technologies to correct grammatical errors and even help with mutations (the system of changing some initial consonants). The Centre for Advanced Welsh and Celtic Studies has published a comprehensive social history of the Welsh language from the early modern period to the present.

Matthew Rhys in his role as poet Dylan Thomas in the film The Edge of Love

There is also a new confidence among young professional Welsh men and women. Although the title of *Cŵl Cymru*, popular at the turn of the millennium, is no longer 'cool', the success of Welsh-speaking artists who have become international stars, such as actors Matthew Rhys, Daniel Evans and Ioan Gruffudd, bands such as the Super Furry Animals and singers Bryn Terfel and Duffy, who are